Angie-The Angel

JAMES FEATHER

WestBow
PRESS
A DIVISION OF THOMAS NELSON

WestBow Press books may be ordered through booksellers or by contacting:

WestBow Press
A Division of Thomas Nelson
1663 Liberty Drive
Bloomington, IN 47403
www.westbowpress.com
1-(866) 928-1240

ISBN: 978-1-4497-3420-6 (sc)
ISBN: 978-1-4497-3421-3 (e)

Library of Congress Control Number: 2012900223

Printed in the United States of America

WestBow Press rev. date: 01/04/2012

Joey's Boo-Boo

CHAPTER ONE

Joey's Boo-Boo

<u>Scene</u>: A Little boy (Age 5) with short light brown hair, and is smaller than most five year olds is coming down three steps of back porch, to enter into the fenced back yard. He is alone and sad. His Nanny just told him that he couldn't ride his toy four wheeler on the street right now, because she didn't have the time to watch him. He is going to the play area in their back yard. The little boy's name is Joey. Joey is going up the ladder of the slide, when he hears a voice:

Angie: "Hi Joey!"

(He stops and looks around to see who is calling out his name, but no one is there. A few seconds later he hears the voice again.)

Angie: "Hi Joey, Can I play with you?"
Joey: "Where are you; are we playing hide and seek?"

(The voice laughs and then all of a sudden a little girl age 5 appears, sitting on one of the swings.)

Angie: "I am sorry Joey; I forget sometimes to appear first before I start talking. My name is Angie!"

(Joey looks at this friendly little girl with yellow hair and smiles and says)

Joey: "How do you do that?"
Angie: "Do what?"
Joey: "How come I did not see you?"
Angie "My Uncle Gabriel taught me how to do that!"
Joey: "What's an uncle?"
Angie: "I am not sure; but I know he teaches me a lot of cool things to do! And he calls himself Uncle Gabriel.
Joey: "My Nanny teaches me lot's of cool things to do too! She teaches me how to make up my bed; and how to tie my shoes, and how to color pictures in my coloring book"
Angie: "Great; maybe she will teach me some things too!"
Joey: "How did you know my name?"
Angie: "My Uncle Gabriel told me your name."
Joey: "Who told him my name? Did my Nanny tell him? Does he live in one of these houses? Where do you live?"
Angie: "I live in heaven!"
Joey: "Is that close to my house?"
Angie: "Very close, it's a really fun place to live!"
Ki`anna: "Who are you talking to?"

(As Angie and Joey turn to see a little African-American girl walking to the swing set. Ki`anna is 6 years old, and lives at the foster home too.)

Joey: "Good morning Ki`anna; did you sleep late?
Ki`anna: "No, its still morning isn't it? Who were you talking to?"
Joey: "I was talking to my new friend Angie"
Angie: "Joey, she cannot see me!"
Ki`anna: "Where is she?"

(Then all of a sudden Ki`anna can see Angie sitting on the swing. It scares her at first.)

Ki`anna: "Yikes!"
Angie: "Do not be afraid; my name is Angie. I am sorry that you could not see me at first, but you can only see me if I want you to!
Ki`anna: "What? How? How did you do that? I did not even see you. You scared me!"
Angie: "I am sorry."
Joey: "This is Ki`anna, she lives in the same house with me. She is six years old and going to school already, we do not have a mommy or daddy; there is just our Nanny!"
Ki`anna: "I am in the first grade. Do you go to my school?"
Angie: "No, I have Uncles that teach me things."
Ki`anna: "What are Uncles?"
Angie: "I am not sure, but they are a lot of fun, and they laugh a lot. They are always happy."

Joey: "Do they ever get sick? I was sick last week, and Nanny made me stay in the bed and take yucky medicine."

Ki`anna: "That's a silly question to ask someone, of course they get sick; everyone gets sick!"

Angie: "I do not know what being sick is, and we do not have beds at my house."

Nanny: "Kids; it's time for breakfast! Come inside and wash your hands please!"

Joey: "Do you want to come and eat with us? We do not have a lot of food, but Nanny will not mind."

Ki`anna: "Yeah; you can have some of my food."

Angie: "Thank you very much, but Uncle Gabriel said to only stay for a little while. Father told me to do everything Uncle Gabriel says."

Joey: "Is your Father mean?"

Angie: "I have the most wonderful Father in the whole world. My Father loves everyone!"

Ki`anna: "Wow! I wish he was my Father!

Joey: "Me too!"

Nanny: "Come on children!"

Ki`anna: "Will you be in our back yard after we eat?"

Angie: "I don't know, but maybe I can stay for a little while."

Joey: "I hope so; you are kind of neat; for a girl!"

Angie: "Thank-you; you better go now before Nanny gets mad at you."

(Then Angie is gone. The two children take a second to stare at each other, and then they race inside the house.)

Joey: "Nanny, Nanny! We have a new friend at the swings!"

Ki`anna: "Nanny, she can disappear!"

Nanny: "That's nice children, wash your hands please."
              "Maria is bringing little Rick over to play with you for awhile. She has to go to the store and buy some food."

Ki`anna: "But little Rick is bad! He is always getting us in trouble!"

Joey: "Nanny; little Rick broke my car last week!"

Nanny: "I know he can get a little excited some times, but remember that Jesus tells us to be nice to everyone."

(The children eat their cereal, and hurry out to find Angie again. Ricardo, called little Rick, shows up with his mother Maria. Little Rick is six years old also. His mother thanks Nanny for watching him for awhile, and leaves him after giving him a hug.)

Maria: "Be nice Ricardo; I'll be back soon."

(As the children go into the back yard, Little Rick races them to the slide.)

Ricardo: "Beat you, beat you; you are too slow!"

Ki`anna: "Angie where are you? Angie!"

Joey: "Angie, are you here?"

Ricardo: "Huh! Who is Angie?"

Joey: "She is a really neat girl who can disappear."

Ki`anna: "Yeah! And she is nice too!"

Ricardo: "You are too old to have make-believe friends:
Let's see who can throw a rock the farthest. I bet
I can hit the side of that house over there."

Joey: "I am not going to throw a rock, Nanny does
not like for me to throw rocks."

Ricardo: "You are just a cry baby! Come on Ki`anna; I
bet I can throw this rock farther than you can
throw another rock."

Ki`anna: "I do not want to throw rocks; I want to find
my new friend Angie!"

Ricardo: "Watch this, maybe I can hit that dog over
there by that tree; I have a good aim!"

Joey: "If you do, I will tell Nanny."

Ricardo: "Here goes, watch this!"

Angie: "Stop! You better not hurt one of Father's
animals; He might get mad at you!"

Ricardo: "Huh! Hey! Where did my rock go? Who said
that? Give me back my rock!"

Ki`anna: "Angie; you are talking before we can see you
again!"

Joey: "Angie! Angie!"

Ricardo: "Who took my rock out of my hand? Where
did it go?"

(Angie appears, sitting on the swing; holding the rock that
Ricardo had, and continues to fuss at Ricardo.)

Angie: You would not like me to hit you with a rock,
would you? That's not being nice!

Ricardo: "That's only a dog! How did you do that? Give me my rock back; don't make me take it from you!"

Angie: "It's time for you to be nice!"

(As soon as Angie spoke those words, Ricardo immediately forgets all about the rock, and throwing it at the dog. Angie has the power to change someone's mind.)

Ricardo: "Hi little girl; where did you come from?

Joey: "She lives in heaven with her Father and Uncles!"

Ki`anna: "Yeah; and they never get sick, or have beds."

Ricardo: "Boy, are you dumb! She would have to be an angel if she never got sick, and lived in heaven!"

Joey: "Are you an angel Angie? Can you fly?"

Angie: "Yes it's true, I am an angel! But I don't really fly; I just go where I want to go!"

Ki`anna: "You really know magic?"

Angie: It's not magic. Father allows me to do special things, so I can let children know that he loves them!"

Ricardo: "I don't want your Father to love me; my dad can take care of me, my Dad is real strong!"

Joey: "I want your Father to love me!"

Ki`anna: "Me too; don't forget me!"

Angie: "My Father loves everyone; even the children who do not want him to love them!"

Joey: "Will you take us to your house to meet your Father?"

Angie: "I am sorry; I cannot take you home with me; only Father can take you to our house! But I will ask him if he will come and visit you!"

Ricardo: "Ha! Ha! Ha! Her Father is Superman! Ha! Ha! Now stop being silly and let's play!"

Ricardo: "Let's race; I am the fastest one in our class at school!"

Joey: "But I am not very fast!"

Ki`anna: "Let's play Soccer; we can play boys against the girls!"

Angie: "Ok, but you will have to teach me."

Ricardo: "It's easy; you kick this ball down the field into the other person's goal, and you get a point. The team with the most points at the end of the game wins!"

Joey: "Yeah; and you do not have to be a ball hog; you can pass it to the other player."

Angie: "Ball hog? You want me to turn into a hog?"

Ki`anna: "Ha! Ha! No silly; he just means not to be selfish with the ball. You are supposed to play together!"

Ricardo: "Boy is this going to be easy! You girls do not stand a chance against me!"

Joey: "Hey! What about me?"

Ricardo: "Yeah! Yeah! If you get the ball, pass it to me and I will go and score!"

Angie: "I have never played this game before!"

Ki`anna: "That's ok; I am pretty good at soccer, we are playing it at school."

(The girls get the ball first. Ki`anna kicks it over to Angie, but before she can touch the ball Ricardo intercepts it and takes it down to the end of the yard. He kicks it between two shrubs.)

Ricardo: "Goal! I scored a goal! I told you this was going to be easy.

Angie: "Did I do something wrong Ki`anna?"

Ki`anna: "No; but next time try to keep them from stealing the ball; Ok?"

Angie: "They did not steal the ball; it is still here in the back yard!"

Joey: "Not that kind of steal; you are not supposed to let us take the ball away from you!"

Angie: "Oh!"

(Angie thinks for a moment, and suddenly yells out.)

Angie: "Hide ball!"

(The ball disappears from everyone's sight.)

Ricardo: "Hey! Where did the ball go? I know it was here a second ago!"

Joey: "What did you do with the ball Angie?"

Angie: "I hid it, so you could not take it away from our team!"

Ki`anna: "Ha! Ha! You sure are a funny girl!"

Joey: "I wish I could do the things that you can do Angie!"

Ricardo: "Give us the ball back; the game is not over yet!"

Ki`anna: "Ok Angie; would you please unhide the ball?"

Angie: "Ball, appear! I am sorry if I did something wrong!"

(As soon as Angie spoke those words, the ball appears in front of the children on the ground at their feet.)

Ricardo: "You cheat! You cannot play that way!"

Angie: "Cheat? What's that?"

Ki`anna: "That's when you don't play by the rules!"

Angie: "What are the rules of this game? I would never cheat. You must always go by the rules!"

Joey: "Don't worry Angie; we are not mad at you! You did not know any better!"

Ki`anna: "Let's try this again!"

(Angie kicks the ball over to Ki`anna, and as she is trying to score against the other side of the yard; Joey gets in her way. She trips and accidentally knocks Joey on the ground. Joey hurts his elbow. It is bleeding a little bit, and he starts to cry.)

Ki`anna: "I'm sorry Joey; I did not mean to make you fall. Are you ok?"

Ricardo: "Ah; he is just a cry baby!"

Angie: "May I see your arm?"

Joey: "No! It hurts!"

Angie: "Please, I will not hurt you!"

(Joey lifts up his arm to show the other kids his Boo-Boo, and Angie gently touches his elbow. The sore is immediately gone, and so is the blood. His arm is just like new.)

Joey: "Wow! Did you see that? The hurt is gone too! Thanks!"

Angie: "You are welcome. Can we play some more?"

Ricardo: "No way, there is something wrong with you! You are a witch or something! I'm going in the house and tell!"

(Ricardo runs into the house.)

Ki`anna: "Don't listen to him; we know you are not a witch, that you are really an angel! We love you Angie!"

Joey: "We sure do!"

Angie: "Thank-you. I have to go now, Father is calling me!"

Joey: "Will you come back later? We like seeing you!"

Ki`anna: "Yeah! Ask your Father if you can spend the night with us!"

Angie: "Ok; but I can't promise anything. Good-bye!"

Joey: "Good-bye; thank-you for fixing my boo-boo!"

Ki`anna: "Good-bye Angie; we will see you later!"

(Angie wants all you children to remember that God loves you very much! Go by the rules when you play games, and always share the ball with each other. Go to Sunday school and Church, and thank God for his love. Learn all about him, and then you can have a relationship with your Heavenly Father.)

Angie Makes a New Friend

CHAPTER TWO

Angie Makes a New Friend

(It is Tuesday, and Ki`anna has just gotten off the school bus in front of her home. As she walks past the Big Oak Tree in the front yard, she hears a voice calling her :)

Angie: "Hi Ki`anna! Did you have fun at school?"

Ki`anna: "What? Where are you Angie? I cannot see you again!"

(Angie immediately appears standing beside her.)

Angie: "Sorry Ki`anna! What did Nanny teach you today?"

Ki`anna: "No, No, Angie! Nanny does not go to my school. I have Teachers that teach me at school."

Angie: "Why does Nanny not go to your school; do they not need her to teach?"

Ki`anna: "Ha! Ha! No Angie; they do not need her!"

Joey: "Ki`anna! Are you talking to Angie?"

Ki`anna: "Yes Joey; I am talking to Angie."

(Angie allows Joey to see her; remember that you cannot see Angie unless she wants you to see her.)

Angie: "Hi Joey! Did you go to school today?"

Joey: "Sure! I do not go to Ki`anna's school; but next year I will! I will ride the bus with her; if we do not have a mommy and daddy by then."

Ki`anna: "Maybe we can have the same mommy and daddy!"

Joey: "I sure hope so! I would really miss you Ki`anna!"

Ki`anna: "Yeah; me too; even though you do come in my room without knocking first! Hey Angie; do you think your Father can help us to find a mommy and daddy?"

Angie: "Sure he can, have you asked him?"

Joey: "Angie; little Rick told Nanny and his mommy about us playing in the back yard Saturday; but they think you are not real."

Angie: "That's ok. Not everyone thinks that Angels are real. Father says that I am to play with children and they tell them that he loves them."

Joey: "Let's go in my bedroom and color pictures. I have a lot of coloring books that are cool. I will let you color in the Spiderman book if you want to Angie, that's my favorite book!"

Angie: "Spiderman? What's a Spiderman?"

Ki`anna: "He is a make believe super hero. He can do a lot of cool things. He saves people from bad guys."

Joey: "Do you know Spiderman Angie?"

Ki`anna: "Spiderman is not real stupid!"

Angie: "You are not supposed to say that word. Why do you need a Spiderman? You have Father!"

Joey: "I do not know how to talk to your Father."

Angie: "Yes you do! You just close your eyes, and think about what you want to tell him, and he will hear you."

Joey: "Will he talk back to me?"

Angie: "Sure he will; but you have to listen for him."

Ki`anna: "We call it prayer; I learned that at Sunday school."

Nanny: "Children! I have you a snack on the kitchen table. Do you have any homework Ki`anna?"

Ki`anna: "No Nanny, they did not give me any today."

Nanny: "Ok honey! You and Joey need to wash your hands before you eat your snack."

Ki`anna: "Ok Nanny!

Joey: "Then we can color in my coloring books, ok?"

Angie: "Ok Joey; but you will have to show me how."

Joey: "Its easy Angie, you just use crayons!"

Ki`anna: "I would rather use markers!"

Angie: "What are crayons? What are markers?"

Ki`anna: "We will show you."

Nanny: "Come on children! I have already poured the milk into your glasses."

Ki`anna: "Angie; there is a new family moving into the house next door. I wonder if there are any kids in the family!"

Angie: "That would be fun; to make new friends."

Joey: "I hope there is a boy for me to play army with."

Angie: "Army? What is army?"

Joey: "It's a cool game you play with army men! Some are lying down, and some are standing up."

Angie: "I have never heard of army Joey."

Ki`anna: "Girls don't play army Angie! That's a dumb game that boy's play!"

Angie: "You are not supposed to say dumb Ki`anna: That is not a nice word!"

Ki`anna: "Ok Angie, sorry; I won't say it any more. But girls dress up their dolls in pretty clothes, and fix up their hair."

Nanny: "Now come on children! I have some great news to tell you."

(Ki`anna and Joey go to the Kitchen table, and sit in their chairs. They have a cold glass of milk to drink and four cookies each.)

Nanny: "Guess what children; there is a family moving in next door. They have two children and both of them are girls."

Joey: "Girls? Oh man!"

Ki`anna: "How old are they Nanny?"

Joey: "I hope they are both fifty; I want a boy to play with!"

Nanny: "I don't know honey, but one looks to be about Joey's age, and the other is about ten or so."

Ki`anna: "Ten years old? Nanny; she is too old for me!

Joey: "Yeah she is really old! She probably drives a car and everything!"

Angie: "Wow! I love making new friends!"

Ki`anna: "You do? Why?"

Nanny: "Were you talking to me Ki`anna?"

Angie: "Because you always learn something new when you make new friends."

Nanny: "Hey look kids; they are in their front yard right now. Do you want to meet them?"

Ki`anna: "Not really! What if they don't like us Nanny?"

Nanny: "They are sure to like you two! You are very special children! Come on, I will go outside with you!"

Joey: "Come on Angie!"

Ki`anna: "Yeah; come on Angie!"

(As Nanny opens the front door, and enters into the front yard; Joey and Ki`anna are close behind her. Angie has turned invisible again.)

Nanny: "Hello girls; would you like some milk and cookies? My children want to meet you!"

(The man that is unloading the big rental truck comes over to the front porch, and he brings the girls with him.)

Mr. Blue: "Hi! We are the Blue family. This is Madeline Blue, and the little one is Lucy Blue. My name is John Blue, and my wife's name is Julie. She is at our old apartment right now packing up dishes."

Nanny: "Welcome to our neighborhood. My name is Susie Smith, and this is Ki`anna, and Joey. They are my foster children! Would you all like some milk and cookies?"

Mr. Blue: "I really do not have the time right now; but maybe my girls would like to stay and play with your children."

Nanny: "Please call me Nanny! I hope you girls will stay and have a snack with Joey and Ki`anna."

Lucy: "Daddy, I want some cookies and milk! Do you have any candy?"

Madeline: "I guess I could have a few cookies; but I do not like milk. Do you have any cola to drink?"

Mr. Blue: "Girls; show this nice lady that you have manners okay? Are you sure that they will not be in your way?"

Nanny: "Not at all; they can eat their snack and get to know each other at the same time."

Joey: "We were going to my room, and color in my Spiderman Coloring book. Do you like to color Lucy? Do you like Spiderman? I have markers too!"

Ki`anna: "Joey quiet down! They are going to have a snack right now. They might not like to color."

Madeline: "No! That's ok; we like to color in coloring books. We do that at our house too!"

Ki`anna: "Really? You don't think it's silly?"

Madeline: "No, even our Mom and Dad color with us sometimes; and we know they are not silly."

Joey: "Spiderman is the coolest ever! He is fighting against the frog man! How old are you Lucy?"

Lucy: "Five; I am five years old! How old are you?"

Joey: "I am five too! And so is Angie!"

Ki`anna: "Come on, this way is the kitchen."

Madeline: "Is Angie your sister?"

Joey: "No. She is an angel who plays with us!"

Nanny: "Now Joey; you behave and let the girls enjoy their snacks."

Lucy: "Angels do not play with boys; only with girls!"

Ki`anna: "You will get use to Joey; he likes to talk a lot!"

Joey: "Do you have an angel at your house too Madeline?"

Madeline: "Yes Joey; our Mom collects angels! She must have a hundred in the living room!"

Joey: "Wow! She has a hundred angels? I want to meet them all!"

Ki`anna: "Hush Joey! You talk too much!"

Nanny: "I am sorry Madeline that we are out of soda; do you like tea?"

Madeline: "Yes ma`am; thank you."

Joey: "We only have one angel!"

Ki`anna: "Finish your snacks and we can go in Joey's bedroom and color."

Joey: "What is that red stuff on your face Madeline? Are you sick?"

Madeline: "No Joey; its called blush! I have makeup on!"

Joey: "Why do you have makeup on, are you in a movie?"

Ki`anna: "Please be quiet Joey!"

Joey: "Is that blush on your lips too?"

Lucy: "She is trying to look pretty for boys. Ha! Ha!"

Ki`anna: "I'm sorry Madeline; I do not know what has gotten into him today!"

Joey: "Let's go and color now."

Madeline: "I am going to help dad to fix my room. He does not know where I want my bed. Your bed is not on this truck Lucy, you stay and color. Thank you for the drink and snack Nanny!"

(Madeline leaves the house and goes into her new house. The other children go into Joey's bedroom and get out the coloring books. They did not even notice that Angie had not been there.)

Lucy: "So where is your one angel Joey?"

Joey: "Angie! Angie, are you here?"

Angie: "Here I am Joey"

(Angie appears sitting on the bed. Everyone including Lucy can see her.)

Lucy: "That was a neat trick; I did not see you hiding behind the bed."

Angie: "I do not do tricks. I am an angel!"

Ki`anna: "Where have you been Angie? I haven't seen you for quite a while."

Angie: "Father had something to tell me."

Lucy: "Do you live here too Angie?"

Angie: "No; I live in heaven."

Lucy: "Stop playing; my daddy told me that there are no such things as angels!"

Ki`anna: "Your daddy was wrong, because she is really an angel!"

Joey: "Yeah! And she can do a lot of cool things."

Lucy: "I'm going home; you children are too silly for me."

(As Lucy tries to get up off the floor in a hurry, she hits the corner of the dresser, and cuts her knee. It is bleeding a little and she starts to cry.)

Angie: "Hold still Lucy! This will not hurt!"

(Angie reaches out and touches Lucy's cut; and the blood and pain are gone. Her knee is as if nothing ever happened to it.)

Lucy: "How? What? Why did you do that? Where is my cut?

Joey: "We told you she was an angel!"

Lucy: "I was not even being nice to you; why did you help me?"

Angie: "Father told me to be nice to everyone all the time!"

Lucy:	"I am going home and tell my daddy how you helped me. I will come back later."
Joey:	"It won't do you any good to tell an old person; they do not believe in angels."

(Lucy leaves in a hurry. Ki`anna is wondering about the prayer that she said the night before.)

Angie:	"Remember when I was gone? Father was telling me something to tell you Ki`anna. He said you talked to him last night, and asked him for a mommy and daddy for you and Joey!"
Ki`anna:	"How did you know what I was thinking? How do you know what I prayed for?"
Joey:	"Her Father told her; have you got crayons in your ears?"
Angie:	"Yes. Father told me. And he also told me that he is going to answer your prayer real soon!"
Ki`anna:	"What does that mean? Is he going to give Joey and me a mommy and daddy?"
Angie:	"Yes; he is!"
Joey:	"Today? Are they here?"
Angie:	"He said that it would be soon."
Ki`anna:	"Why would your Father do that for us? We are poor and cannot give him anything!"
Joey:	"Tell him I will give him my Spiderman Book!"
Angie:	"Father loves you! And he does not want your Spiderman book. He only wants you to love

him too! I have to go home now, Father told me to tell you to keep talking to him."

Ki`anna: "Tell him that I do love him!"

Joey: "Me too; tell him thank you for not taking my Spiderman book. Your Father really is the best!"

Ki`anna: "Bye Angie!"

Joey: "Bye Angie; we love you too!"

Ki`anna: "We sure do!"

Angie: "Bye Joey and Ki`anna; I love you too!"

(God wants you to talk to him too! Pray and ask him to be your Father in heaven; and don't be afraid to meet new friends.)

A Special Friend

CHAPTER THREE

A Special Friend

(As the children are in their bedrooms, Nanny sits down to watch the afternoon news on the television. She hears a big truck backing up, and it sounds like the truck is in her front yard. She gets up and looks out the window on her front door. There is another moving truck backing up to the house across the street. She wonders who is moving in there.)

Nanny: "I didn't know that any one was even looking at Mr. Brown's house, much less moving into it!"

(She realizes that no one heard her, and thinks to herself; I heard that as you get older, that you start talking to yourself. The thought tickles her and a big smile comes to her face.)

Nanny: "Children; come here please. There is another family moving in across the street!"

Ki`anna: "Do you see any children with this new family?"

Joey: "Yeah! Any boys to play army with?"

Nanny:	"Not so far; I have only seen two men and one woman."
Joey:	"I don't think that Lucy likes me Nanny."
Nanny:	"You must not think that way honey! A new friendship takes time: you do not meet someone and instantly become friends."
Ki`anna:	"Instantly means right away Joey!"
Joey:	"But I loved Angie inseantly Nanny!"
Nanny:	"Baby; I am talking about real people, and not make believe friends."
Ki`anna Whispers:	"Hush Joey! We know that Angie is real, don't we?"
Joey:	"Very real Ki`anna! But Angie is not very good at soccer."
Ki`anna:	"It's ok Joey! I do not think that angels play soccer where they live."

(Nanny notices that Lucy is sitting on her bicycle in the front yard of her house. She suggests that Joey go over there and ask her if she wants to play in their back yard.)

Nanny:	"I need for you Ki`anna, to come and help me in the laundry room for a few minutes."
Ki`anna:	"Joey; go and get Lucy to come over and play with us! I will first help Nanny!"
Joey:	"Ok Ki`anna; but I do not think she likes me."

(As Ki`anna follows Nanny into the laundry room, Joey runs over to Lucy's house to where she is sitting on her bicycle.)

Joey: "Do you want to play in our back yard?"

Lucy: "I can't play with you no more today! My Daddy said that because I told a lie, that I am being punished."

Joey: "You told a lie?"

Lucy: "No Joey; I told daddy about Angie fixing my knee, and he got mad at me!"

Joey: "But Angie did fix your knee."

Lucy: "Daddy does not believe me."

Mr. Blue: "Lucy; come inside and help Madeline fix up her bedroom."

Lucy: "Yes Daddy! Bye Joey!"

Joey: "Bye Lucy!"

Lucy: "Maybe I can play with you tomorrow!"

(As Lucy goes into her house, Joey slowly walks back to his own house, and meets Nanny in the doorway.)

Joey: "Nanny; why do old people not think that angels are real?"

Nanny: "Old people? Do you mean grownups?"

Joey: "You know; Mommies and Daddies and Nannies."

Nanny: "I am a Nanny; and I believe in angels!"

Joey: "But you do not think that Angie is real, do you?"

Nanny: "Honey; there are angels in heaven right now helping God with his work!"

Joey: "I only know Angie!"

(Nanny is interrupted by the telephone ringing. She leaves Joey and answers the phone.)

Nanny: "Hello! May I help you? Oh; hi Mrs. Blange! The children are doing great! There is a family that is interested in both children? Oh; I won't say anything to the children! They are renting the house across the street? They want to get to know the children first? Is that safe? Oh; you have already checked this family out carefully? What do you want me to do? Act like I do not know what's going on? We are going to have a meeting on Monday while the kids are in school? Okay Mrs. Blange! I will talk to you then. Thanks for the information! I promise that I will not say a word to the children! Goodbye!

(Nanny sits back down in her chair in the living room; and she is feeling all kinds of emotions. One moment she is sad at the thought of the children living in someone else's house; and then she feels excited that they could possibly have a Mommy and Daddy for the rest of their lives. Afraid that the children might see her tears, she tries to think about something else; but she has had these two children for a long time now. She has been taking care of Joey for two years, and she received Ki`anna one and a half years ago. She has such a strong love for them both, and doesn't know how to react to this news.)

Joey: "Nanny! Can I go out back and swing?"

Nanny: "Ok Joey!"

(Nanny reaches out and hugs Joey tight)

Nanny: "You know that Nanny Loves you very much, don't you?"

Joey: "Sure I do Nanny! I love you too! Do you want to come and swing with me?"

Nanny: "I sure do Joey; but only for a few minutes. I have to do laundry."

Ki`anna: "I'm going too! I have finished all my chores."

(Nanny reaches and grabs Ki`anna softly; and hugs her for a couple of minutes.)

Joey: "She done that to me too!"

Ki`anna: "Why did you hug me Nanny?"

Nanny: "Because I love you Ki`anna!"

(Unable to hold back her tears another minute; Nanny races off and runs into the bathroom and closes the door.)

Joey: "Wow! I never seen Nanny run before; she must have to tee tee real bad!"

Ki`anna: "Yeah! Let's go see if Angie is on the swings."

(The children did not notice that Nanny was crying; and they run outside to the swing set.)

Joey: "Angie! Where are you?"

Ki`anna: "Hi Angie; let us see you!"

(But there is no Angie at the swing set in the back yard.)

Joey: "Maybe Angie is in the front yard."

(Ki`anna and Joey race through the house and go out into the front yard yelling for Angie.)

Joey: "Look Ki`anna; there is a boy over there."

Ki`anna: "Yeah! I guess he is going to live in that house across the street. He is older than Madeline."

Joey: "Yeah! I bet he is too old to play army with me."

(The boy notices the two children staring at him; and comes across the street towards them.)

Joey: "Uh oh! Should we run Ki`anna?"

Ki`anna: "No Joey; he does not look like he is mad or anything."

Ashton: "Hello! My name is Ashton. What are your names?"

Joey: "My name is Joey."

**Ki`anna:** "I am Ki`anna"

Joey: "Do you like army?"

Ashton: "Huh? Army? Sure; I guess army is ok!"

Joey: "Will you play army with me?"

Ashton: "Sure; but today I have to help my parents move stuff into this house. Maybe I can find time later! Do you go to church?

Ki`anna: "Yes; we ride the church bus every Sunday morning! Our Nanny drives her car, but does not ride the bus with us."

Ashton: "What kind of church do you go to?"

Joey: "It's a big church, with a lot of children in it."

Ki`anna: "It's not very far; only around the corner."

Joey: "They are teaching us about a man called Jesus!"

Ashton: "I know Jesus! And I think that you are going to that big white church that we passed coming over here. Can I ride the bus with you?"

Ki`anna: "You will have to ask Mr. More; he is our church bus driver. But he is always telling us to bring a friend with us; so I am sure that he would not mind."

Joey: "You can be my friend!"

Ki`anna: "Mine too! Maybe we can invite Lucy and Madeline too!"

Ashton: "That sounds like a great idea! I have to get back to work now, but I will see you in a little while!"

Ki`anna: "Ok Ashton!"

Joey: "I will go and get all my army men out and have them ready!"

Ashton: "Great idea! Bye now!"

Ki`anna: "Bye!"

Joey: "Bye; hurry up and come play with me!"

(Ashton then goes back across the street and into his house. The children go back into their house all excited.)

Ki`anna: "Nanny; we made another friend. His name is Ashton, and he is going to ride the church bus with us tomorrow."

Joey: "But first he is going to play army with me."

Nanny: "That's nice children. He sounds like a very nice friend."

(The children go into their own rooms again. Ki`anna wants to be alone so she can pray; and Joey wants to get his army men laid out across his bed.)

Ki`anna's prayer: "Hi Angie's Father. I know that I am new at this praying stuff, but thanks to Angie I know you really do hear me. Thank you for letting her come and play with me and Joey. She needs more practice with her soccer, but she sure is nice; and we love her too. Angie's Father; she told me that you are going to bring me and Joey a new mommy and daddy. I am very happy to know this and I promise to be a good girl for them; will you help me? Thank you for our new friends. See you at church tomorrow! Bye Angie's Father!

(Nanny has gone into the kitchen to start making supper. She is wondering how so much could happen in only one day. With two new families moving in the neighborhood; one of which might adopt her foster children; when the door bell interferes with her thoughts. She goes to the front door.)

Nanny: "May I help you?"

Ashton: "Yes ma`am! My name is Ashton. I am the son of Carlos and Betty Rodriguez. We are moving into that house across the street. I met your children and promised to play army with Joey; if you don't mind of course!"

Nanny: "My name is Susie, but I like to be called Nanny!"

Ashton: "Yes ma`am! I have heard a lot of really good things about you! It is my pleasure to meet you."

Nanny: "You have? Well it's my pleasure to meet you also young Ashton! Come on in; Joey is in his bedroom. I will show you where the bedroom is."

Ashton: "Thank you ma`am! I know that it will soon be time for supper; so I will not stay too long."

Nanny: "Ki`anna told me that you plan to go to church with them tomorrow. We attend a Christian church, and the bus gets here around 9:30 in the morning."

Ashton: "Thank you for the information. I will be ready and waiting outside at 9:30."

Joey: "Hi Ashton!"

Ashton: "Hi Joey! Wow! That is a lot of army men."

(Nanny goes back into the kitchen feeling a lot better now that she has met this nice and polite young boy. Mean while Ki`anna has a guest come visit her in her room.)

Angie: "Hi Ki`anna! What are you doing?"

Ki`anna: "Hi Angie! I just talked to your Father a few minutes ago. Did he hear me again?"

Angie: "Yes he did Ki`anna. He said that you do not have to call him Angie's father; you can call him heavenly Father. Do you like your new friend Ashton?

Ki`anna: "How did you know about Ashton? Were you out there with us?"

Angie: "No; I was with Father, and he told me his name. Father said that you are going to have a lot of fun with Ashton. I have to help Father for awhile, so I cannot stay. Maybe I can go to church with you tomorrow!"

Ki`anna: "I sure hope so Angie; I like it when you are here! Bye!"

Angie: "Bye Ki`anna: I will be back as soon as I can."

(Nanny has just about got supper ready, and goes and asks Ashton if he would like to join them. Ashton thanks her but says that he and his parents have more things to go and get from their other house.)

Ashton: "Ok Joey; I have to go home now. I had a lot of fun playing army with you.
See you in the morning. Bye!"

Joey: "Bye Ashton. Thank you for helping me pick up all those army men."

Nanny: "Nice meeting you Ashton. Tell your parents that I am looking forward to meeting them

also. See you tomorrow. Wash your hands
children and come and eat please."

(After Ashton has left, and the children have washed their
hands; they all sit down to their plates at the kitchen
table.)

Nanny: "Who wants to say our prayer tonight?"

Ki`anna: "I do Nanny! Let me please!"

Nanny: "Go ahead Ki`anna; close your eyes Joey."

Ki`anna's
prayer: "Hi again Father! Angie told me to call you
that; is it okay? I want to thank you for us
having food. Thank you for our Nanny. Thank
you for Joey. Thank you for our new friends!
And thank you for our special friend Angie!
Bye now!"

Nanny: "That was a very nice prayer honey; I am sure
that God liked it."

Ki`anna: "Is that who Father is; God?"

Nanny: "That's who my heavenly father is."

Ki`anna: "Wow! I did not know that I was talking to
God!"

Joey: "You talked to God?"

Ki`anna: "Yeah! And he has been hearing me too!"

Joey: "God has ears like me?"

Nanny: "I want you to try to understand something
children. Yes God hears us, and he answers
us too? But God is not like us; he is a Spirit,
a very powerful Spirit who made all things,

so be careful what you say when you talk to him!"

Ki`anna: "All things? Even bad things?"

Joey: "Did God make mean dogs?"

Nanny: "God does not make mean dogs; but he make's dogs! And sometimes people make dogs mean. Do you see the difference?"

Joey: "Why do people make dogs mean?"

Nanny: "Oh boy! Let me try again. Not all people make all dogs mean; only a few dogs are mean. Most dogs are nice! Eat your carrots before they get cold honey!"

Ki`anna: "And Angie said that Father does not like for us to throw rocks at dogs either!"

Joey: "But Little Rick does!"

Ki`anna: "Not when Angie is here he don't!"

Joey: "That's for sure!"

Nanny: "Ok children; finish eating and we will color tonight in coloring books if you want to."

A New Family

CHAPTER FOUR

A New Family

(As Ashton enters his house, his parents are eager to hear his thoughts about how he feels about Joey and Ki`anna.)

Carlos: "Well son; what do you think about the children?"

Ashton: "That Joey is a trip! I really enjoyed playing army with him. I did not get to spend any time with Ki`anna, but I plan to tomorrow. I told the kids that I would ride the church bus with them tomorrow; is that alright?"

Betty: "What kind of church do they attend?"

Ashton: "Nanny said that it was a Christian church! You are going to like Nanny. I believe that everything that we heard about her is true. She seems like a very nice person! She said that she was looking forward to meeting you both."

Carlos: "I believe that our lives are fixing to be blessed greatly, with our future very bright!"

Betty: "I have so much wanted small children running around our house; our children! I feel as though God is going to answer our prayers!"

Carlos: "I think he has already done that; but I would love to have more children!

(As they continue to put things away in their rental house; across the street Nanny and the children are coloring in their coloring books. In the blink of an eye, it is Sunday morning. The children are ready for church, and go out on the front porch to wait for the church bus.)

Joey: "Look; here comes Ashton!"

Ki`anna: "Yeah; and he is all dressed up!"

Ashton: "Good morning Ki`anna and Joey. Can I wait for the bus over here with you?"

Joey: "Sure Ashton! Sit here with me."

Ki`anna: "Hi Ashton; you look neat this morning!"

Ashton: "Thank you Ki`anna; you look pretty yourself. Joey, you look handsome!"

Joey: "I hope they have a puppet show in Sunday school today! I like that lion puppet!"

Ki`anna: "We go to children's church Ashton. Sometimes they have a puppet show."

Ashton: "That sounds pretty cool Ki`anna; what is the lions name?"

Joey: "His name is Stanley; Stanley the lion!"

(Then they notice the church bus coming towards their house. They also notice the Blue family leaving their house, and everyone is dressed up.)

Ki`anna: "Look Joey; I think Madeline and Lucy are going to church too!"

Joey: "Our church? They could ride the bus with us!"

Ki`anna: "They might not be going to our church Joey."

Joey: "Why not?"

Ashton: "Not everyone goes to the same kind of church Joey; there are all kinds of denominations!"

Joey: "What's that? That you said?"

Ashton: "People believe different meanings to God's word. They also worship a little different!"

Joey: "What did you say?"

(Their conversation is interrupted by a man's voice; "Are you riding the bus or not?" They had not even noticed Mr. More parked in front of the house with the bus door open.)

Ashton: "Sorry sir! May I ride with my new friends to visit your church?"

Mr. More: "Welcome aboard son! We are always receiving new friends at our church! My name is Mr. More."

Ki`anna: "This is Ashton, Mr. More, and he is my friend!"

Joey: "Mine too! Don't forget me!"

(Ashton is glad for the interruption. He was getting himself in a fix with his conversation about Denominations to Joey. He now realizes that he must be more careful about talking religion to children. They can get confused easily, and religion can be very difficult to understand. Ashton wonders himself why there are so many kinds of churches; considering that there is only one God! They are in front of that white church in no time, and it is the church that Ashton mentioned to the children yesterday. Mr. More shows Ashton to his classroom. The children go to the fellowship hall where the children's church is held.)

Ki`anna: "I like Ashton; do you Joey?"
Joey: "Yeah! But he talks with funny words."
Ki`anna: "Look! There's Angie!"
Joey: "Where? I do not see her."
Ki`anna: "Sitting up front in my chair!"
Joey: "I see her; let's hurry!"

(The children run to where Angie is sitting, but a grown up tells them to slow down.)

Angie: "Hi Ki`anna! Hi Joey!"
Joey: "Hi Angie! Can anyone see you?"
Angie: "Yes Joey; everyone can see me!"
Joey: "Even old people?"
Ki`anna: "Stop calling people old; they are grownups!"
Angie: "Even grownups Joey! They do not know that I am an angel; they only see me as a little girl. Let's not tell them our secret for now ok?"
Joey: "Ok Angie, if you say so. But you do not meet an angel every day!"

(Joey is dishearted because he cannot tell everyone that Angie is really an angel. Ki`anna is happy that Angie is there sitting with them. She talks to Angie all through Children's Church. On the ride home Ashton wonders why Joey is so quiet.)

Ashton: "Are you alright little buddy?"

Joey: "No; I finally meet an angel after all these years, and she won't even let me tell anyone!"

Ashton: "All these years? Joey, you are only five!"

Joey: "You see what I mean?"

Ashton: "Oh yeah Joey; definitely! Why is Ki`anna in the back of the bus; and who is she talking to?"

Joey: "The angel that I am not allowed to tell you about!"

Ashton: "Oh; that angel! Now I see!"

(While the boys carry on their conversation; the girls are talking also.)

Ki`anna: "I had a great time today Angie; thank you for going to church with us."

Angie: "I had a great time too! I liked those songs too! Why was Joey so quiet? Is he getting sick again?"

Ki`anna: "No. He is mad that you would not let him tell everyone that you are really an angel!"

Angie: "Oh! I did not want to make him mad at me!"

Ki`anna: "That's ok Angie; I make him mad at me all the time! He gets red in the face; and I think he's cute!"

Angie: "Father does not want us to make other people mad at us. He says we are to be nice all the time."

Ki`anna: "Ok Angie; I will try not to make anyone mad at me anymore. But what if I do make someone mad at me by accident?"

Angie: "Ask Father to forgive you, and then ask him to help you to not do it again."

Ki`anna: "What does forgive mean?"

Angie: "That means to not be mad anymore at someone who has made you mad!"

Ki`anna: "Huh? Not be mad when I am mad? How do I do that?

Angie: "You better ask Father to help you; but it is easy if you do not get mad in the first place!"

Ki`anna: "I would like to never get mad, but I do not know how to do that!"

Angie: "Maybe if you practiced to be happy all the time; then maybe you would not get mad! I have to go now; but I will see you soon! I love you Ki`anna."

Ki`anna: "Bye Angie. I love you too!"

(Ki`anna joins the boys in front of the bus.)

Ashton: "Did you enjoy your conversation with your angel Ki`anna?"

Ki`anna: "You could see Angie?"

Ashton: "No! Joey told me about your angel."

Joey: "I did not tell anyone; only Ashton!"

Ki`anna: "How does a person never get mad Ashton? Angie said that to forgive is not being mad when you are!"

Ashton: "Wow! That's a super question! Unfortunately I do not know how to never get mad. I really wish that I did, because my life would be a lot better if I could do that! Sometimes I get mad and say things to hurt someone's feelings because they hurt mine first! Then I wish that I had not done that!"

Joey: "I told you he uses funny words."

Ki`anna: "Be quiet Joey; I want to learn this! Angie said to ask her Father for his help."

Ashton: "Who is Angie's father?"

Ki`anna: "Why God of course! She is an angel!"

Ashton: "Of course! That was a stupid question! I am sorry."

Joey: "You are not supposed to say stupid; that is not a nice word."

Ashton: "You are so right my man! I can learn a lot from you two!"

Joey: "And Angie too! She is the smart one!"

(They find themselves in front of the children's house. Ashton can hardly wait to talk to his parents. He tells the children goodbye and hurries home. The children go towards their front door where Nanny is waiting for them.)

Nanny: "I barely beat you children home! Did you have a good day at church?

Joey: "Not really; I was not allowed to tell my secret!"

Ki`anna: "It was great; I got to sit with a special friend."

Nanny: "Secret? Joey, a secret is something that is supposed to stay inside of the one who has it. You are not supposed to tell anyone about your secret. Change your dress clothes while I find us something to eat for lunch."

Joey: "Ki`anna; Nanny sounds just like Angie!"

(While this family is settling down for lunch; there is a lot of excitement across the street.)

Ashton: "Mother, I must speak to you!"

Betty: "What is wrong Ashton? Why are you yelling?"

Ashton: "Mom; you must help me talk Dad into getting these two children as part of this family! They are so awesome! I want them as my brother and sister!"

Carlos: "What's going on in here? You can hear your voice down the street Ashton!"

Ashton: "Sorry Dad! I am just so excited! Dad; please get these children into this family!"

Carlos: "Calm down son; I haven't even met these children, and you want me to adopt them! This is a very serious decision that I cannot make rashly! We have to make sure that God

is in this move in our life; and also wait on him
to provide!"

Ashton: "Ok Dad; but you will see that it only takes
one time being with them and you will love
them too!"

Betty: "Maybe we could take them all to lunch at our
restaurant Carlos!

Carlos: "Great idea Betty! Have Ashton run across the
street and invite them."

Betty: "You know; I am almost as excited as Ashton,
and I have not even met these children!"

(Ashton is in his bedroom. He is about to change his
clothes, but first wants to talk to God. He gets down on
his knee's to pray.)

Ashton: "Dear God! Thank you for the service at church
today! Thank you for letting me spend time
with Joey and Ki`anna. I know it was only for
a few minutes; but it seemed more like hours.
Will you please talk to my Dad and Mom,
and help them to see that we need those kids
in our family? They are so awesome! Help their
Nanny too! Thank you God for being such a
great God! I love you! A-men.

(Just then his mother Betty knocks at his door.)

Ashton: "Come in!"

Betty: "Ashton; go over to the children's house, and ask Nanny if we can please treat them to lunch at father's restaurant."

Ashton: "Really mom? Thank you!"

(Ashton fly's out the front door, and is knocking on the children's front door in only minutes. He tells Nanny about what his parents want to do, and Nanny accepts their invitation. Nanny knows that they are trying to get to know the children, and does not want to interfere.)

Nanny: "Children! Put your dress clothes back on! We are going to a restaurant with the family across the street."

Joey: "But Nanny; I just took them off!"

Nanny: "I know honey, but Ashton's mommy and daddy want to buy our lunch!"

Joey: "We are eating lunch at the grocery store?"

Nanny: "No baby! Get dressed and you will learn what a restaurant is, ok?"

(Soon the two families are entering the restaurant by the name "Carlos' Place". The host shows them to their table and gets their drink order. The children are amazed at what they are seeing. They have never been in a restaurant before. Carlos and Betty are more nervous than anyone.)

Carlos: "How do you like this place Ki`anna?"

Ki`anna: "This is neat place sir! But only a little cold!"

Joey: "Are all these people your family Ashton?"

Ashton: "No Joey; they are called customers!"

Joey: "There he goes again Ki`anna, with those funny words!"

(The waiter interrupts them with their drinks, and asks if they are ready to order their meal yet. Carlos asks the waiter to bring the manager to their table. In only a few minutes the manager is standing in front of them.)

Manager: "May I be of assistance to you folks?"

Carlos: "Hi Philip! Yes; this lovely child said that it was a little cold in here. Would you be kind and fix this problem please?"

Philip: "Oh Mr. Rodriguez; I was not told that you and your family would be attending our establishment today! I will take care of this immediately sir; is there anything else that I may do for you today?"

Carlos: "Not at this time Philip; thank you for your quick response!"

Philip: "Oh yes sir; and may I say what an honor it is to have you all here with us today!"

(As the manager leaves to go and adjust the thermostat, Joey notices how fast he is in leaving.)

Joey: "Nanny! He must have to tee-tee real bad; just like you did yesterday!

Ki`anna: "Quiet down Joey! But he was in a hurry though wasn't he!"

(While everyone is laughing; Nanny is feeling good about this family and the future of her foster children.)

Ashton: "Ki`anna; what would you like to eat. You can order anything in that menu that you want to!"

Ki`anna: "I want my Nanny to order my food please!"

Joey: "Me too Ashton! I do not see any pictures in this food book; and I cannot read yet on account of my only being five years old. Do they have peanut butter and jelly sandwiches here?

Carlos: "No Joey they don't; but if that's what you want, then I will have Philip go to the store and get that for you?"

Joey: "No that's ok! They might not have any money for peanut butter or jelly; I can eat some-thing else!"

Betty: "Joey; I promise that this restaurant will have peanut butter and jelly sandwiches the next time you come in here!

Carlos: "It sure will; my entire restaurant's will as of tomorrow!"

Nanny: "How many restaurants do you have Mr. Rodriguez; if you do not mind me asking?"

Carlos: "Please call me Carlos Mrs. Smith! We have four in operation, and three in construction at this time! I must tell you what God has placed on my heart; and I know that this is highly irregular! We have a very large house; with seven bedrooms not even being used. Is it possible for you and the children to come and stay with us for awhile, so that we can all get to know each other better? There will be no stipulations attached and you may leave with the children whenever you like! I will make the payments on all your bills, and give you a handsome salary. Betty can take the children to their schools and kindergarten, and pick them up every day. Talk to God and give me an answer when you feel right to do so!

Nanny: "Wow! That is highly irregular Mr. Rodriguez; I mean Carlos! Please call me Nanny! I will talk to the children tonight and see what they have to say; and we all need to pray and seek God's will for us all."

(Nanny and the children agree to live with the Rodriguez family; and within six months the children are being adopted by Carlos and Betty. Nanny stays on as the children's Nanny and remains with the family also. Angie visits the children often, but father has another child that Angie must help. Look for Angie's new friendship in the coming future; and re-member that God loves you very much and wants you to talk to him every day. God has sent you his son to be your friend! His name is Jesus! Get to know him!)

Meeting Little Kim

CHAPTER FIVE

Meeting Little Kim

Scene: (Class room in an Elementary School; first grade teacher Mrs. Broom is introducing a little brown haired skinny girl, who is very pretty and is the age six to the class).

Mrs. Broom: Class; this is Kim. She has just moved here from another state. Say hello to Kim, Class!

Class: Hello Kim!

Kim: Hello class, I am happy to meet you!

(A boy sitting in one of the desks up front yells out)

Bobby: Why does she talk funny?

Mrs. Broom: That is called an accent! She is not from the south!

Bobby: Where is she from? Another planet?

(The class room is filled with laughter, and Kim becomes very nervous).

Mrs. Broom: Calm down class. Very funny Bobby. Turn in your school books to page 16. Kim; you may sit in that desk in the third row!

(Kim goes and sits in the desk that Mrs. Broom is pointing to, right beside a little boy).

Frank: Hey Kim! Don't pay no mind to Bobby; he is a mean boy. My name is Frank!
Kim: Hello Frank!

(Mrs. Broom speaks out in a stern voice to Frank).

Mrs. Broom: I do not see your book open Frank!
Frank: Yes ma'am Mrs. Broom; sorry bout that!

(Kim looks around the classroom at the other children and wonders if she will make any new friends. All of a sudden a piece of pencil hits Kim in her back. She turns to see a girl laughing at her).

Vicki: My maw says that girls with yellow hair are dumb!

(Then the boy sitting next to Vicki speaks out).

Andrew: She may be dumb; but she shore is perty! Don't like that dress though!

(Kim thinks to herself that she really misses Kindergarten).

Vicki:	That dress looks like it belongs to her mama!

(Kim is very skinny and her dress is a little too big for her; but she only has three dresses and she has to wear it. The rest of the day the children stare at Kim, and no one talks to her. On the ride home from school, she sits by herself on one of the seats on the school bus; then suddenly she hears a voice).

Angie:	Can I sit with you?
Kim:	Yes; if you want to! Are you going to make fun of my dress too?
Angie:	No; I like that dress!
Kim:	You do? Why?
Angie:	I love to look at flowers; my Father does too!
Kim:	I don't have a father; mother said that he went to a place called heaven!
Angie:	That's where I live!
Kim:	You do? Do you know my father?
Angie:	No' but my Father does!
Kim:	Where is heaven? Can I go with you?
Angie:	Sorry Kim; only my Father can take you to heaven, but I will ask Father to come and visit you!
Kim:	Okay; my name is Kim!
Angie:	My name is Angie!

(The bus stops at a little blue house with a big tree in the front yard, and the bus driver calls out Kim's name).

Kim:	This is my grandmother's house. Mother and I live here with her. Do you want to come over and play?
Angie:	Yes, I would love to play with you. I can come now if you want me to!
Kim:	But how will you get home?
Angie:	My Uncle Gabriel will come and get me!
Kim:	Great! We can play catch. I have a glove and a softball!
Angie:	Catch? You will have to teach me catch!
Kim:	Will you be my friend Angie? I do not have any friends; and the kids at school do not like me!
Angie:	I am your friend! Kim, all the children at school are not bad; only some of them are!

(A voice calls out to Kim as soon as she reaches the porch).

Grandmother:	Don't get that dress dirty Kim; you are going to have to wear it again tomorrow. My washing machine broke today; sorry honey!
Kim:	That's alright grandmother; can we have a snack?
Grandmother:	We? Who is with you? I do not see anyone else!

(Angie makes herself visible to grandmother. Remember that no one can see Angie unless she wants them to).

Grandmother: Oh! I'm sorry honey; I did not see you. You must have been behind our tree!

(Before Kim can say anything; Angie speaks quietly to Kim).

Angie:	Kim; I need to tell you something!
Kim:	What is it Angie?
Angie:	Do you know what an angel is?
Kim:	Sure silly! It's a person with wings!
Angie:	They do not all have wings, and I am an angel!
Kim:	You think that I am dumb too? I know that angels are not real! That's not funny Angie!

(Angie disappears from Kim's sight, and re-appears on the front porch).

Kim:	How did you do that? How come I did not see you run to the porch? Do you know magic?
Angie:	It's not magic Kim! I told you that I am an angel!

(Just then grandmother comes out the front door of the house, and joins the girls on the front porch).

Grandmother:	Little girl; do you like chocolate cake?
Angie:	I think so; I have not eaten chocolate cake!
Kim:	Her name is Angie grandmother; and she thinks that she is an angel!

Grandmother: That's nice honey! I guess that there are two little angels on my front porch! Come in and have your snack, okay?

(Just then a car pulls into Grandmothers driveway. The car is making a loud rattling sound. In a few moments a woman with brown hair is walking towards the house.)

Grandmother: Hi Sweetie; did you have any luck with your job interview?

Sherry: No ma'am! They said that they could not use me!

Grandmother: Baby; I do not know how we are going to pay for our electricity!

Sherry: I'm sorry mom; but I am trying to get a job. No one seems to be hiring right now!

Kim: Angie; that is my mother Sherry. She is trying to get a job.

Angie: Would it help your mother if she had a job?

Kim: Yes, very much!

Angie: I will ask Father to send your mother a job.

Kim: No Angie; you do not get jobs in the mail; never mind; let's go eat our snack.

(Before the girls can get into the house; Grandmother grabs her chest and leans over on the handrail that is on the porch).

Sherry: Mom! Are you okay?

Kim: Grandmother! Are you sick?

(Angie reaches over and touches Grandmother on her side and Grandmother stands up straight).

Grandmother: I'm ok now; the pain is gone. It must have been gas!

Angie: Grandmother is not sick anymore Kim!

Sherry: Don't do that Mom! You scared me!

(After they eat their snack, the two girls go outside with the glove and the softball).

Angie: This ball is smaller than the ball that Joey and Ki'anna play with.

Kim: Who are they? Is that your brother and sister?

Angie: No; they are my good friends!

Kim: Do they live close to my house?

Angie: No; they live a long way from here. They showed me how to play soccer!

Kim: Oh yeah! Soccer does use a much bigger ball than catch; but you can use that ball too! With catch you throw the ball, and you do not kick it!

Angie: Where do you throw it? Not at dogs I hope!

Kim: No! No! Angie; you throw the ball to each other, and you also catch it!

Angie: Why do you do that?

Kim: I do not know; because it is fun I guess!

Angie: I have to go now, Father is calling me and Uncle is waiting!

Kim: Where? I do not see him!

(Kim turns to look around the yard, and notices that Angie is gone).

Grandmother: Kim, I forgot to ask you if you have any homework!

Kim: No ma'am Grandmother. Grandmother; do you believe in angels?

Grandmother: I sure do! I know they are real because they are mentioned in my Bible!

Kim: Do you think that someday, you would read to me you're Bible?

Grandmother: I would love to! We will start tonight after supper. I suppose that we also need to find us a church to visit on Sunday!

Kim: What is a church?

Grandmother: It's a place where people gather together to worship God, Jesus, and the Holy Spirit. You can also learn what is said in the Holy Bible as well!

Kim: Who are God, Jesus, and the Holy Spirit? Are they mean?

Grandmother: No baby they are not mean; although they can show anger! Honey, God is the one who made everything that you can see; and also everything that you cannot see. Jesus is God's only Son, who came here to die on the cross to become our sacrifice to God for our sins; and the Holy Spirit is the one who lives inside of us, those who believe and accept Jesus Christ. He also guides us through life here on earth!

Kim: Huh? I do not know what you just said Grandmother!

Grandmother: Don't worry honey! I will teach you slowly so that you can understand everything!

Kim: What do angels look like? Don't they have wings?

Grandmother: I have always thought that angels look like you and me. I do not know if they have wings or not. Maybe we can find out together as we read in my Bible!

Kim: I do not understand! Do you think that Angie could be an angel Grandmother? She can disappear!

Grandmother: Maybe honey! I do believe that angels are real. Watch and see how she acts. Angels are close to God! They cannot sin like we can. They also have special powers to do whatever God has told them to do!

Kim: Sin? What is sin?

Grandmother: Oh boy; I could use a preacher right now. Honey; sin is when you do something that God has told you not to do!

Kim: Have I sin? I have never heard what God tells me to do!

Grandmother: Don't worry honey; we will learn all these things together. I can see that we need some Sunday school also. Does your mother pray with you at night before you go to sleep?

Kim: She sure does grandmother. Now I lay me down to sleep. I pray the Lord my soul to keep. If I should die before I wake, I pray the Lord my soul to take! God bless mommy, grandmother, and everybody! A-men!

Grandmother: Very good honey! Do you understand what all those words mean?

Kim: No Ma'am! But I like the way that it sounds.

Grandmother: After supper; you and I are going to talk to your mother.

Kim: What about Grandmother?

Grandmother: It seems that your mother has forgotten some things that she learned in church when she was about your age. I think that she needs to be reminded of all these things.

Kim: Grandmother; where is heaven?

Grandmother: That's where your father lives!

Kim: Angie said that her Father knows my father!

Grandmother: That's sad! She must have lost her father too.

Kim: No Grandmother! Her Father talks to her. She said that she lives in heaven too!

Grandmother: She would really have to be an angel if she lived there! We will talk to her next time we see her; and ask her what kind of church she attends. I do not want you to hear any false doctrine.

Kim: Huh? What is dockerine?

Grandmother: Doctrine is books that you are taught out of!

(As the Grandmother and Kim walk into the house to get ready for supper; Kim is thinking about all the things that Grandmother has said. As they enter into the kitchen, Sherry is sitting at the table drinking a glass of tea).

Grandmother: Sherry; I need to talk to you about something very serious.

Sherry: What about Mother?

Grandmother: Why are you not taking your child to church, or teaching her anything about our Lord Jesus?

Sherry: Mother: we are poor! I do not have a husband, and I do not have a job! I do not have tithe money, a nice dress, and my car would probably scare half of them to death! What church would welcome me or my child?

Grandmother: I'll tell you what church would welcome you and your child. A real God fearing church! One that worships and loves God in truth! A Christian church that would be humbled and honored that you are there!

Sherry: Get real Mother! There are three churches within walking distance of this house; Christian churches. Have you ever had anyone to visit you and invite you to come and worship with them?

Grandmother: No! But that is not the point! I have never gone to any church because I was seeking for them to accept me. I have always gone because it is a temple of my God and my creator!

Sherry: Ok Mother; we will start going to church! You can pick out which one that we can visit.

Grandmother: After supper, I am going to start teaching Kim, with God's help of course, about the Bible; or at least what little that I know about it! You are invited to join us if you like.

Sherry: You know Mother; my life is going nowhere right now; and I could use a little help from God! I am going to join you and Kim!

Grandmother: Now that sounds more like the child that I raised up.

(As they eat supper together, Grandmother is humming a song.)

Kim: Grandmother; you are not supposed to play at the kitchen table.

Sherry: Kim; show your Grandmother some manners.

Grandmother: No Sherry; the child is right. I am not supposed to play at the kitchen table. You are a smart young lady.

Kim: Thank-you Grandmother; but I do not think that I am old enough to be a lady.

(Sherry and Grandmother cannot help but laugh at Kim's remark.)

Better Days

CHAPTER SIX

Better Days

(It is Tuesday morning and Kim is slowly getting ready for school).

Grandmother: Kim; honey, you need to hurry up and get ready or you will miss your school bus.

Kim: I don't want to go to school Grandmother. The children don't like me.

Grandmother: Sure they do honey; what's not to like?

Kim: But they make fun of my dress!

Grandmother: I'm sorry Kim, but you have to go to school. As soon as I can, I will buy you a new dress okay?

Kim: Okay Grandmother.

Grandmother: What about your new friend? Does she sit in any of your classes?

Kim: You mean Angie? She did not sit with me in class yesterday, only on my bus ride home.

Grandmother: At least you have a friend to ride with you to school and then home again. Let's go honey; here comes the bus.

Kim: Okay Grandmother.
Grandmother: I love you honey!
Kim: I love you too Grandmother!

(As Kim gets on the school bus, she does not see Angie anywhere. She sits down on a seat by herself).

Angie: Hi Kim, how did you sleep?
Kim: Huh? Angie? Where were you? I did not even see you hiding.
Angie: Hiding? I was not hiding. I was sitting here and waiting for you!
Kim: What church do you go to? My Grandmother wants to know.
Angie: Church? I will go to your church!
Kim: I do not go to church yet, but Grandmother said that we are going to find one.
Angie: I will go with you when you do find one.
Kim: Angie; where is heaven?
Angie: It's very close to your house; only you cannot see it!
Kim: Then how can you live there? How do you find it when you go home?
Angie: Because Father does not want you to see it yet, but some day you will. It is like me! When I do not want you to see me, then you don't!
Kim: I do not understand any of this. Who is your father Angie?
Angie: Father has a lot of names; but I just call him Father!

Kim:	I do not know your Father Angie!
Angie:	I know you don't Kim; but he sure knows you!
Kim:	Have I met him?
Angie:	Not yet Kim; but you will! Your Grandmother knows him.
Kim:	She does? She has met your Father?
Angie:	That's what my Father told me, and I believe him; he never lies!

(Kim does not even notice that the other children are making fun of her).

Boy:	Hey stupid! Who are you talking to?
Kim:	I am talking to my friend Angie!
Boy:	Is Angie a ghost?

(The other children laugh out loud and Kim feels tears come to her eyes. All of a sudden the boy slips out of his seat and falls on the floor. The children are now laughing at him instead of Kim. Even Kim gets a little happier).

Boy:	Stop laughing at me! Who pushed me?

(Just then the bus comes to a stop and the driver says "Ok kids, we are here!")

Angie:	Do not worry about the other children; I will be with you today!
Kim:	Don't you have to go to your class?

Angie:	Class? My school is not here where your school is, and I do not learn the things that you learn. Father is giving your Mother a job today.
Kim:	Really? My Mother is going to work for your Father?
Angie:	No; not yet! But she will work for Carlos.
Kim:	Who is Carlos?
Angie:	He is one of Father's children. Joey and Ki'anna live with him and Nanny too!
Kim:	Huh? I do not know what you say sometimes Angie; but I believe you are my friend!

(Kim notices that all the other children are not making fun at her, so she decides to listen to the teacher. Meanwhile, there is a phone call at Grandmother's house).

Grandmother:	Hello; may I help you?
Tim:	Is this Sherry Johnson?
Grandmother:	No, hold for just a moment and I will get her.
Tim:	Thank-you Ma'am!
Grandmother:	Sherry; wake up! This phone call is for you.
Sherry:	Hello?
Tim:	Is this Sherry Johnson?
Sherry:	Yes it is; how may I help you?
Tim:	This is about your employment application at Carlos'. If you are not employed yet, I would like to set up an interview!

Sherry:	No sir! I mean yes sir! I mean I am not employed and would like to have an interview.
Tim:	I am available at 11:00 this morning, is that ok with you?
Sherry:	Yes sir; thank-you! I will be there! Bye!
Grandmother:	What was that about?
Sherry:	I don't know Mother! I applied at that Restaurant two weeks ago, and the Asst. Manager told me that they could not use me. This is probably going to be a waist of time, but at least I have somewhere to start my day!
Grandmother:	I am glad you joined Kim and me for Bible reading last night. I am going in my room and pray that God will help you find a job today!
Sherry:	Thanks Mother. I am glad I joined the two of you also; and thanks for the prayers.

(Sherry wears her best dress for her interview with this Tim fellow. As she pulls into the parking lot at Carlos' Restaurant, she is greeted by a tall man with jet black hair. It appears he works out quite often, looking at the size of his stature).

Tim:	Are you Sherry? My name is Tim McClure.
Sherry:	Yes sir! How are you today?
Tim:	Good thank-you! Do you want a job? I want to train you to be our floor manager!

Sherry: Please tell me that you are not teasing me!

Tim: I never tease at work! Is that a yes or no?

Sherry: I don't understand! Two weeks ago, your Asst. Manager told me that you could not use me, and now you say you want to train me to be a floor Manager?

Tim: Let me apologize for my behavior. I do not mean to be in such a hurry! We send applications to the owner's house, even though we do our own hiring. Every now and then, he chooses someone he wants to do certain positions. This is the case with you. I have been instructed to not only hire you, but to see to your training personally. Also, you are instructed to go and lease a vehicle of your choice at our expense. He will talk to you himself on Friday to arrange your pay, and answer all of your questions!

Sherry: Who will talk to me? I'm sorry, but all this is highly ill regular.

Tim: Carlos will be in touch with you. He has his reasons for doing this. If I were you; I would accept his offer and be very thankful! That car dealership across the street is expecting you this morning. Everything has already been taken care of. Training will start at 6:30 a.m. tomorrow morning. Is it a deal?

Sherry:	Yes sir! And thank-you! I will work very hard!
Tim:	When you go to the dealer, ask for Johnny.

(Tim gets into his car and pulls away. Sherry does not know what to think, but goes across the street to the Car Dealership. As she gets out of her car, a woman asks her if she can be of assistance. Sherry asks to speak to Johnny. In a few moments a man walks up to her).

Johnny:	Can I help you Ma'am?
Sherry:	I'm not sure. Tim from Carlos' Restaurant told me to ask for you.
Johnny:	You must be Sherry! I have been instructed to set you up with a lease on one of these new vehicles!
Sherry:	I am afraid that this so-called car of mine is all I have to offer you for a trade in.
Johnny:	You do not need a trade in, this is a lease contract! Come inside my office and I will explain everything.
Sherry:	I do not have a down payment either.
Johnny:	This way please; everything is paid for!

(Within hours, Sherry is pulling into her Mother's driveway in her new car).

Grandmother: What's this child? Where did you get this car?

Sherry: You are going to have to sit down Mother. You are not going to believe my day; in fact, I'm not sure that I believe it!

(Sherry tells her Mother all about her interview and what Tim told her. When she finishes telling her story, she hears the brakes of the school bus and looks outside to see Kim walking towards the porch. She hurries out to greet her child filled with excitement).

Sherry: Honey; you are not going to believe this!

Kim: Did you get your job yet Mother?

Sherry: Huh? Yes I did, but how did you guess?

Kim: Angie said her Father was going to give you a job. A man named Carlos hired you didn't he?

Sherry: I really don't believe this!

Kim: Are you happy Mother?

Sherry: Yes baby I am! Who is Angie? How could she possibly know these things?

Kim: Angie is my friend. She knows a lot of things!

Sherry: It does appear that way!

(Sherry has to sit down on the front porch. She is confused by all that has happened today, and her child who was in school seems to know all about it).

Grandmother: Hey Sherry; did you tell Kim about your job and car?

Sherry: I didn't have to Mother, a girl named Angie told her. Who is Angie?

Grandmother: Angie is Kim's' new friend. They like to go out back and play catch.

Sherry: Is this Angie one of Carlos' children?

Grandmother: Maybe? I really don't know anything about her except that she thinks that she is an angel!

Sherry: An angel? Wow! Of all the things that a child can imagine themselves to be, you would never think of a child wanting to be an angel.

Grandmother: True; she must have some awesome parents. I'd like to meet them!

Sherry: I want to meet Angie!

(Grandmother and Sherry go into the house and look out the window in the kitchen; where they can see in the backyard. There is Kim and Angie playing catch and laughing).

Grandmother: She is a beautiful girl isn't she?

Sherry: She sure is. Her hair is the same color as the sun is!

Grandmother: Would you like to meet her?

(Just then the telephone rings).

Sherry: Hello?

Carlos: Is Sherry Johnson available to talk?

Sherry: Yes sir; this is Sherry Johnson speaking.

Carlos: Hi Sherry; I am Carlos of Carlos' Restaurants. I wanted to set up a meeting with you on Friday; but another situation has come up and I need to leave town for a couple of days.

Sherry: I totally understand sir.

Carlos: Do you like your car?

Sherry: Oh yes sir. Thank-you very much! Will the payments be payroll deducted?

Carlos: No; the car is my gift to you, and your family. I don't suppose your husband Bob mentioned me in his letters to you when he was in the army?

Sherry: He did mention a Carlos then; but he didn't say much. Are you possibly the same Carlos?

Carlos: Yes Ma'am I am. So you know that we were best friends! I'm sorry that he passed away.

Sherry: Thank-you for your sympathy. But I do not understand all the kindness.

Carlos: Bob and I made a deal while we were at war. If one of us did not make it back home, then the other would help to take care of his family.

Sherry: But Bob was killed in a car accident, by a drunk driver.

Carlos: Yes Ma'am I know; but our deal was also for life. I loved Bob as a brother, and I mean to do my part for you and your family.

Sherry: There is no-way that I can repay all your kindness.

Carlos: Yes there is! You can do your best as a mother, and raise Bob's daughter to be a good person; one who knows and loves God!

Sherry: Yes; God has been coming up a lot these past few days! I promise you right here and now; that I will do my part. Thank-you for all of your kindness!

Carlos: Please allow me to do my part. I would like to invite you and your daughter to come to my residence and meet my family! God has recently blessed me with two more children of my own; oh yes; and a Nanny!

Sherry: We would love to meet your family sir; you just say when!

Carlos: Learn as much as you can as one of my floor managers, and when I get back in town, we will get our families together. Betty also wants to meet you; she's my lovely wife.

Sherry: By chance, do you know an Angie? A little girl about five or six?

Carlos: No; I am not aware of an Angie. My children may know her though. Joey is five, and Ki'anna is six. Well, it's been nice talking to you, if you need anything, let my manager Tim know. Have a nice day; oh, by the way; your clothes are also

	taken care of, both you and your child at my cost. A check is in the mail as we speak!
Sherry:	Sir; what can I say beyond thank-you?
Carlos:	I will be in contact soon. Take care of yourself, and your family. And don't forget to thank our God!
Sherry:	Yes sir! Bye!

(Sherry did not notice that Grandmother had gone outside to get the mail while she was talking on the phone. She enters the room as Sherry is saying goodbye.)

Kim Gets New Clothes

CHAPTER SEVEN

Kim Gets New Clothes

(The rest of the week goes by quickly. Angie continues to be with Kim, and Kim plays with Angie after school. Grandmother has become curious about Angie and where she came from. Sherry is learning to be a floor manager at one of Carlos' restaurants where Tim is her manager.)

Grandmother: What a beautiful Saturday morning this is. It's going to be a wonderful day. Good morning Sherry.

Sherry: Good morning Mother! I couldn't agree more about this beautiful day. Let's take a picnic lunch over to the park and watch the kids play in the playground.

Grandmother: That sounds great. If you can get her out of the bed that is; she must have been worn out. Look; the mailman is at our mailbox. He sure comes early on Saturday.

Sherry: I'll grab the mail if you will wake up our sleeping beauty.

(Sherry is only gone for a couple of minutes because their front yard is small, and the mailbox is not a long distance away. In fact their big Oak tree takes up most of their front yard. Grandmother is making coffee when she hears Sherry come back into the house).

Sherry: Mother; when I talked to Carlos on the phone the other day, he told me that he was sending us a check to help out with clothes for us. But this check is way too much for clothes, he must have made a mistake!

Grandmother: How much is it for? You know that we are having to go to the laundry place to clean our clothes now because our washing machine has decided to retire.

(As Sherry shows Grandmother the check, she has to sit down at the kitchen table. With this check being far more than either of them could have imagined.)

Grandmother: I'm talking to that adorable little Angie if she comes today. There is far too many good things going on here, then we could ever deserve. God has to be behind all these wonderful things.

Sherry: You think so Mother? We have been ignoring God for so long; that I know I do not deserve anything good from him!

Grandmother: He truly is a forgiving and loving God! He won't be getting ignored around my

	house any more. I have chosen the church that we will be attending tomorrow.
Sherry:	Great! We need to go to the clothing store today and buy some nice new clothes. Sunday clothes! You know that Carlos must really have loved Bob, to show us so much kindness.
Kim:	Clothing store? Can you get a biscuit there, because I am hungry Mother?
Grandmother:	Do my eyes deceive me? Or has sleeping beauty arisen? Good morning honey!
Kim:	Are they going to be big on me? The kids at school make fun of my dresses because they are too big for me.
Sherry:	No, my darling; these new dresses are going to look like they were made just for you.
Kim:	Grandmother; I like the story about Jesus that you read to me last night; can you read some more tonight?
Grandmother:	It would be my pleasure honey. Did you thank him in your prayer last night for your new friend Angie? Is she coming over today?
Kim:	I did thank God for my new friend Angie; but I don't think he was listening to me, because I was real quiet so that I could hear him, but I didn't hear him say you're welcome.

(Sherry and Grandmother cannot help but laugh in joy at how adorable their little Kim is.)

Sherry: God always hears us honey, but we do not always hear him. Now go get dressed and we will go by a restaurant and get us a biscuit on the way to the clothing store.

(So Grandmother, Sherry, and Kim all go into their bedrooms to get dressed. Kim is looking for her blue jeans that she thinks are under her bed, when she hears Angie talking to her.)

Angie: Hi Kim, what are you looking for?

Kim: Hi Angie; I am looking for my blue jeans! Grandmother, Mother, and me are going to a restaurant for a biscuit, and then I am going to get a new dress today! Do you want to come with us?

Angie: I have to go visit my Joey and Ki'anna today, but maybe I can come to see you some today.

Kim: Your Father is really nice! He not only gave Mother a job, but I think she also has new friends too!

Angie: Father told me to tell you that you are welcome!

Kim: He really did hear me last night?

Angie: Yes Kim, he heard you! In a little while, you are going to meet my friends Joey and Ki'anna. You will really like them.

Kim:	Today?
Angie:	No, not today, but soon! Tell Grandmother that I would love to sit down and talk to her.
Kim:	Huh? You saw Grandmother this morning?
Angie:	No Kim! Please tell her that message; she will understand what it means.
Kim:	Okay Angie, but you can tell her if you want to, she is only in her bedroom.
Angie:	It's time for me to be going. I will see you later Kim. Bye.
Kim:	Bye Angie! I will see you later!

(Angie disappears out of sight right before Kim's eyes. Kim knows in her heart that Angie really is an angel, whatever an angel is.)

Sherry:	Let's go family! We are burning daylight!
Grandmother:	Wow! A week ago we could not even pay our light bill, and now we are going to buy new clothes. Thank-you God!
Kim:	What's a light bill Grandmother?
Grandmother:	That's a bill we get in the mail so we can have electricity.
Kim:	Does everything come in the mail Grandmother?
Grandmother:	It's true that a lot of things do come in the mail honey, but not everything does.
Kim:	Grandmother, Angie told me to tell you that she would love to talk with you. I

think she really is an angel. She can be
here one moment and then she is not
there!

Grandmother: I'm afraid that I am ready to agree with
you honey.

(Kim cannot remember a day in which she has had so
much fun. She has five new dresses, two pairs of shoes,
new pretty panties, and even new socks. Mother also
bought Grandmother a new washing machine and dryer.
By the time that they get home, she is very tired.)

Kim: Mother; I think that this is the best day
ever! Thank you for all my new clothes.

Sherry: I wish that I could take the credit for all
that has happened today; but this day
is a result of our heavenly Father, and a
sample of his grace!

Kim: What did you say? I do not know what
you said.

Sherry: God is sometimes called the Heavenly
Father! Because he lives in Heaven, and
he is the Father over all things! Now when
you pray tonight, do not forget to thank
God for all your new clothes.

Kim: Yes ma'am. I missed Angie today.

(Sunday was an exciting day for Grandmother, Sherry,
and Kim. They visited a church that is close to Grand—
mother's house, and got to meet a lot of really nice people.
Kim learned about a man named Noah, who made a really

big boat! He and his children had to go and get a whole lot of animals to stay on the boat with them. Then God made it rain for 40 days and 40 nights. When it stopped raining, Noah and his family were the only people that were alive on the earth. But now it is Monday morning, and Kim is getting ready for school; and still no Angie.)

Kim: I hope that Angie goes to school today Grandmother. I want to tell her what fun we had at church and at the clothes store too!

Grandmother: You did not see her any this weekend?

Kim: No ma'am. You do not think that I made her mad at me, do you?

Grandmother: No honey, I imagine that she was probably real busy and did not get a chance to come. You have a fun day at school honey.

Kim: Yes Ma'am. I bet no one makes fun of this dress Grandmother.

Grandmother: I bet they do not make fun of it either!

(While Kim is riding to school, she notices that the children are all looking at her, but no one is saying anything to her. The day at school goes by real fast, and now Kim is getting off the bus at Grandmother's house. Kim is walking towards the front porch, when she is startled by a voice.)

Angie: Hi Kim. Did you have a good weekend?

Kim: Hi Angie! I can hear you but I cannot see you. Where are you?

(Angie appears, walking beside Kim).

Kim: Angie; you are not going to believe what Grandmother, Mother, and me did this weekend. We had so much fun! I wish you could have been there with us.

Angie: I have a lot of time, so you can tell me all about it, okay?

Kim: Oh yes; I will be happy to tell you. Angie; are you really an angel?

Angie: Yes I am!

Kim: Are you the one that is giving us all these new things?

Angie: No Kim; Father is giving you all these new things. He wants you to be one of his children!

Kim: How can I be one of your Father's children?

Angie: Father told me that soon he is going to come and visit you. You will know what to do then!

Kim: Why does your Father want to visit me? Why is he being so nice to me?

Angie: Because he loves you Kim! And he only wants you to love him too!

(Grandmother interrupts the girls' conversation. The girls have been sitting on the front porch talking).

Grandmother: Do you have any homework today honey?

Kim: No ma'am.

Grandmother: Did you see Angie today at school?

Kim: Grandmother, Angie is sitting right here beside me; do you not see her?

(Angie makes herself visible to Grandmother; and Grandmother quickly gets down on her knees in front of Angie).

Grandmother: Oh my precious God, you really do have angels!

Angie: Father says to get up Grandmother! You are not supposed to get on your knees for me, only for him!

Grandmother: I'm sorry; I just wanted to show you reverence. I am so blessed to be in your presence Angie, that I am not sure how that I should act!

Angie: Act like yourself. I am only one angel. Father has many, many more. I have been sent to give Kim a true friend.

Kim: You are my friend Angie. I love you!

Angie: And I love you too. I love Grandmother and Mother too!

Grandmother: Angie; how can we possibly re-pay God for all of his kindness?

Angie: He says to obey the words that are written for you in his book. And teach Kim also! You will be friends of Joey, Ki'anna, and

	their new family. They will help you, but do not forget Father anymore! It's time for me to go Kim. I will come and visit you sometimes. Goodbye Kim. Goodbye Grandmother.
Kim:	No! Don't leave me Angie! Please stay with me! I love you!
Grandmother:	Goodbye Angie; and thank-you so much!
Angie:	You are welcome. There are many more children who need a true friend Kim! You will see me again. We will always be friends.
Kim:	Wait Angie; I want to talk to you some more.

(But Angie fades out of sight of Kim and Grandmother. Tears roll down their faces as they look at each other. As a couple of weeks go by, many changes occur. The kids at Kim's school are no longer mean to her. Sherry has learned her new job and Grandmother is pleased with the new church that they are attending. She really loves the fact that Jesus is now back in her families eyes and they are seeking to please him. Kim will soon meet Jesus. Do you know Jesus? He sure knows you!)

Kim Meets Joey and Ki'anna

CHAPTER EIGHT

Kim Meets Joey and Ki'anna

(Another week has passed and Kim has not seen Angie. She is thinking about her when she hears the phone ringing. Her mother Sherry answers the phone.)

Sherry: Hello? Hi Tim! You say that Carlos has arranged for my family to eat with his family for supper? Yes, we would love to come. Thank you for calling!

Grandmother: Who was that Sherry?

Sherry: It was my manager mother. It seems like we all have a dinner date with Carlos' family tonight at our restaurant. He has given me the day off with pay!

Grandmother: I don't know if my heart can withstand any more blessings, I am already overflowing with joy!

Kim: Mother; is Carlos the father of Joey and Ki'anna?

Sherry: I think those are their names, but how do you know these things Kim?

Kim: Angie told me that I would meet them and that they would be my new friends.

Grandmother: Well; if Angie said that, then we know that those things will come to be.

Sherry: What do you two have going on between you and this Angie child?

Kim: I got to go and get ready, maybe Angie will come there too!

Sherry: Mother; if I didn't know better, I would think that Jesus has totally taken over our lives!

Grandmother: Is that a bad thing Sherry?

Sherry: Mother; I have never been happier in my entire life! How did we ever live without him?

Grandmother: Not very well my daughter; not very well at all!

(The day seemed to fly by and the Johnson family with Grandmother enters into Carlos' restaurant. Sherry's other floor manager meets them at the entrance.)

Linda: Hi Sherry. Mr. Rodriguez and his family are waiting on you in the V.I.P. room. I did not know that you were friends with them!

Sherry: You never know who might turn out to be your friend Linda.

(As Grandmother, Sherry and Kim walk towards the table in which Carlos, Betty, Nanny, Joey, and Ki'anna is sitting, their excitement is hard to control).

Carlos: Welcome everyone; I am glad you could make it.

Sherry: We are more than honored to be asked to come and have supper with you and your family sir.

Joey: Angie told us that you were coming.

Kim: You know Angie?

Ki'anna: Angie is our best friend!

Kim: Mine too!

Betty: Children, why don't you go into the play area and we will order your supper for you.

Joey: Okay but I want the Joey special please.

Kim: What's the Joey special?

Ki'anna: A peanut butter and jelly sandwich, a bag of potato chips, and a large glass of chocolate milk. Yuck!

(As the children go into the inside play area, the grownups are now free to have a conversation).

Nanny: Joey loves to talk, but he is an amazing child.

Grandmother: We have one of those children as well.

Carlos: Is everything going well for you Sherry?

Sherry: Yes Sir Mr. Rodriguez! I don't know how I will be able to ever repay you!

Carlos: Your husband Bob gave me friendship when I needed it most. It is I who cannot repay my debt!

Betty:	Carlos never wrote me a letter in which he did not brag on their friendship Sherry. Bob must have been a wonderful man. I am so sorry for your loss!
Sherry:	Yes, he really was! I rely on the fact that one day we will be together once again in Heaven.

(Carlos, Betty, Grandmother, and Nanny say Amen. While the adults get to know each other better, the children are also talking when they get an unexpected visitor).

Joey:	Do you go to school Kim?
Kim:	Yes, but I don't like it very much.
Ki'anna:	Boy, I do! I really like making new friends.
Kim:	I do not have any friends, except Angie!
Joey:	We have a friend Angie too. She is an angel!
Ki'anna:	Quiet Joey!
Kim:	My friend Angie is an angel too!
Angie:	Hello everyone!

(The children recognize Angie's voice but no one can see her).

Ki'anna:	Angie; we hear you but we cannot see you.

(Angie appears on the top of the slide).

Angie:	Sorry Ki'anna. I forgot again.

Joey and Kim: Hi Angie!

Joey: Where have you been Angie? It's has been many years since we have seen you?

Ki'anna: Joey; we saw her last weekend!

Joey: You see what I mean?

Angie: Sorry Joey, but Father has been teaching me about the Bible.

Kim: Grandmother has been teaching me about the Bible too Angie!

Ki'anna: Are you going to eat supper with us Angie?

Angie: No Ki'anna. I have to go meet a new friend.

Joey: But you could eat a Joey special if you could stay!

Angie: Next time I will eat a Joey special with you Joey okay?

Joey: Ok Angie, but your tummy is going to be very mad at you!

(Angie says goodbye and then disappears from their sight).

Joey: I am worried about Angie Ki'anna!

Ki'anna: Why Joey?

Joey: Because she is working much too hard. She is only a little angel.

Kim: She did not even play with us this time.

Ki'anna: We should pray and ask her Father to maybe give her a vacation.

Joey: I sure do love her!

Kim: Me too!

Ki'anna: Yeah, me three!

(Nanny comes into the play area but did not see that one of the balls had rolled over by the entrance and she steps on it and falls to the ground.)

Joey: Nanny; are you okay?
Ki'anna: Are you hurt Nanny?

(Nanny, who gets up laughing calms down the children).

Nanny: I'm fine children! It takes more than a little ball to keep me down!
Joey: Kim; Old people are always falling down.
Kim: Old people?
Ki'anna: He means adults. Stop calling them old people Joey!
Joey: I'll try Ki'anna, but they sure look old to me!
Nanny: Okay Joey. You and the girls come inside and eat with us old people!

(The dinner seems to go by fast with everyone really enjoying themselves. Kim now has two more very good friends in Ki'anna and Joey, and they spend a lot of weekends together having fun and getting to know each other. Angie visits each of them from time to time, but God has another child who he wants Angie to meet).

Look for more adventures of Angie in the future. Remember that God loves YOU so much that he sent his only Begotten Son JESUS to come and take away your sins, if you will only believe in him and then let him into your heart!

I am so blessed that the Lord placed this play/book on my heart. I was raised in a Christian Church until I was the age of nine, and had been baptized, but it wasn't until I was 43 years of age and was diagnosed with Leukemia that I really came to know Jesus as my Lord and Savior. The Lord not only saved my soul from my sins, but also healed my body without me ever having to take any treatments. I have been so thankful for God's Love and Grace, and Jesus' sacrifice on the cross for me, that I want to share Jesus' Testimony with this world and showing them where they too can receive God's Love and Grace!

The Lord has written a Devotional Book using my hands and it is named "Message's From Heaven Above". He has also written 45 Poems through my hands and many Sunday School Messages that for the past five years I have been blessed to share them with the Adult Men's Class at the church that I am a member of.

This play/book is hopefully going to bring many who are lost in their sins to the Lord Jesus Christ! I pray that you have both enjoyed the Love within this play/book, but also that you are inspired to go and show some kindness to others, and don't forget to tell them what Jesus did for them also, if they would only receive his Salvation!!!

CPSIA information can be obtained at www.ICGtesting.com
Printed in the USA
LVOW111839150412

277647LV00001B/1/P